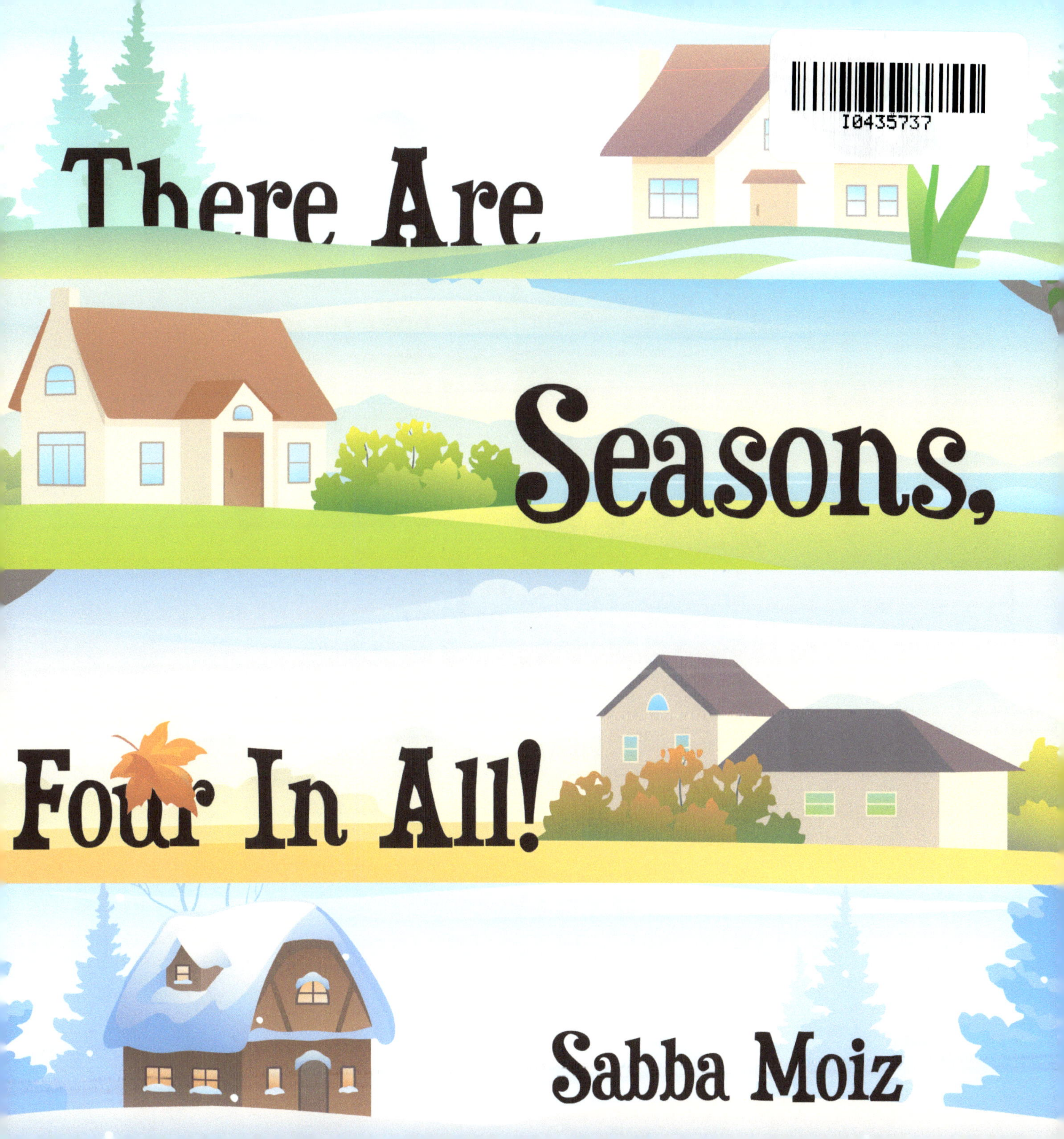

# There Are

# Seasons,

# Four In All!

## Sabba Moiz

Rev. date: 11/26/2013

To order additional copies of this book, contact:
Xlibris LLC
1-888-795-4274
www.Xlibris.com
Orders@Xlibris.com

# There Are Seasons, Four In All!

# Dedication Page

I dedicate this book to all the youngsters in the world and my husband, who believed that I can do anything and supported me in every step of the way.

# Table Of Contents

# Fall

# Fall

The leaves turn colors.
Red, yellow, green, and brown
the wind blows and they all fall down

# Winter

# *Winter*

The world turns white.
Cold chilly breezy days
The snow is cold and it falls wet and light

# Spring

# Spring

Colorful flowers blooming

Raindrops falling

Trees growing

Spring is coming, Spring is coming

# Summer

# Summer

The sun makes the outside a warm place to play

Days full of fun

Beaches, Parks, Swimming and plenty of sun to play all day

*Winter*, *Spring*, *Summer*, *Fall*

Which Season Do You Like Of Them All ??

# About The Author

Sabba Moiz, born and raised in Brooklyn, New York. She lives in Elmont, New York with her husband and two kids.